Blood Moon

JANE BLUE

FUTURECYCLE PRESS
www.futurecycle.org

Copyright © 2014 Jane Blue
All Rights Reserved

Published by FutureCycle Press
Hayesville, North Carolina, USA

ISBN 978-1-938853-44-9

To my husband, Peter Rodman

Contents

I: ARGUMENT

A Drive in the Country	9
Parallel Universes: Villanelle	11
End of Summer	12
Argument	13
Attachments	14
Ghazal of the Cyanide Almond	15
Fiat	16
Sometimes an Angel	17
Ghazal of the Broken Heart	18
Butterfly Wings and Honeybees	19
Identity Theft	20
A History of Navigation	21
The Dressmaker	22
I've Known You So Long, I Don't Know You	23
Scenes from Outside and Inside the Asylum	24
Bernini's Ecstasy of St. Teresa	26
In the Bleak Midwinter	27
Courage	28

II: ENGLISH USAGE

Sword-Swallower	31
Oak Gall	32
An Anagram of Love	33
Praying Mantis	34
English Usage	35
The Pink Violet and the Thesaurus	36
Necessary Dissonance	37
Rudolf Serkin's Hands	38
Typewriter	39
Dogs of the City	40
A Morning During the Tour de France	42
Testing the Floodgates	43

III: THE SHOWER AT CARMEL

The Cooler 47
The Shower at Carmel 48
Architecture 49
Returning 50
Is Everybody's Father a Fiction? 51
Your Mother Never Dies 52
Fog 53
The Piano 54
Another Fiction 55
The Body of Pangelinan Cruz at Land's End 56
Remembering Carmel in Texas 58
Through the Sealed Windows 59
The Week After Easter 60
Ladybug 61
Refuge 62
Two Weeks in September 63
Chicory and Rue: Ghazal 64
Blood Moon Seen Through Cataracts 65
The End of the World 66
Acknowledgments

I: ARGUMENT

A Drive in the Country

1

That early, false spring. A crape myrtle
sways in a gentle downpour. The pink camellia
nooked into the yard is blooming. I always see
instead the white camellia of another marriage.

It's as though I've lived two lives simultaneously,
one buried in the past, continuing
in all its drama to be etched onto the present one.
An overpowering odor of violets, escaped

into the lawns. The deep pink of ornamental plums
and Japanese magnolia, opening satin cups
to a cold sun. Who are we, after all,
under our skin?

2

We receive the gas bill in the mail, a blow
harder than the cold winter.
We worry more about the expense
of love. How it fades,
where it blooms anew. How it sends out tendrils,
crawling, like the violets. He prunes,

killing when necessary; I weed, plucking grasses
from the flower beds. We communicate through roots.

3

A string of holidays like leftover Christmas lights.
We pass the time with movies,
a drive in the country, and the specter
of love at our throats.

Almond trees just budding.
Against black clouds they seem phosphorescent
like a gas. All along the roadside
so many fat hawks in bare trees.

At home the heavens open. I hear
near thunderclaps, the crash
of hail, ice-clots on the metal awnings.

Parallel Universes: Villanelle

A sparrow zooms perpendicular into an ash tree;
leopard markings, a black head, and it's gone.
Fledgling doves zigzag, suspended, through the street.

An empty hearse glides by, from some secret fleet.
Sparrows skitter, singing their cacophonous, atonal song.
One zooms perpendicular into an ash tree.

Pablo Neruda was tendered a toy wooly
lamb through a fence's hole. He returned with a pine cone.
Fledgling doves zigzag, suspended, through the street.

It surprises me that the boy was still there to receive it.
As though they lived in parallel universes, alone.
A sparrow zooms perpendicular into an ash tree.

It's how old lovers live, parallel, never to see
one another again except bobbing above hedgerows,
as fledgling doves zigzag, suspended, through the street.

We bleed and we slough skin and we heal, particles free
and recombining, eternally done and undone.
A sparrow zooms perpendicular into an ash tree.
Fledgling doves zigzag, suspended, through the street.

End of Summer

1

In July's long heat wave we felt
we were dead, or we were the living dead.
We had no hunger, no hungers.
We couldn't wail. We couldn't smell
or even taste. But now, the aroma of coffee,
the door open, traffic shushing by.
A phone ringing, jazz, blues, gospel in the air.
A fly examines my flesh
for rottenness—grease, dirt, any way in.
It's cold enough in the morning now
to change the trees quickly
like adolescence.

I like the way the sky opens in winter—
another month or two; I expect to live
to see it. But who knows? Who ever knows?

2

The Rose of Sharon, the crape myrtle, opulent;
fat and messy at the end of their season.
I love them. They are a part of my life.

I have lived in this place longer than anywhere,
even childhood.

I am planted here, yet every day I think about moving.

Argument

One crimson blossom of the Rose of Sharon peers
through the kitchen window, little hibiscus
of late autumn.

What do you say?

That beauty is random: you must look at it
and seize it. That life goes on.

The sun so bright, ash leaves glitter as they fall.

Beauty is not random. It belongs to the young.

Beauty is like a gun to your head. Beauty
is like a ravaging disease.

Life does not go on. The leaves are piled, swept
into dull mounds in the street, like
biers, like cairns.

Halloween: fog comes, obscuring the fake
cobwebs and gigantic spiders
crawling up the children's houses.

Let beauty fall on you as the sun
that even above the fog is there. And at night,
the moon to reflect it.

The moon is dead.
Only the sun brings forth its beauty.

Attachments

For Michael

He sleeps under a dark sky in Idaho, alone with the stars.
In the empty part of Washington, he writes, he's seen the Milky Way
thrown against the sky.

I walk to the café, where I write. A leaf falls in my hair.
Green acorns roll out thick on the broken sidewalk. A dove
shoots up into my periphery.

When people touch each other in public, I look away—
out to the lamb clouds and the green-leaved ash and the swath
of blue sky. They are so young

being clothed means nothing. There's a window between us now.
She leaves. He raises his bare muscled shoulders above his head.
The clouds recede

feathering into shapes. Two heads swirl, leaning
sensuously away from each other, postcoital, dissolving.

A barista is killing flies.

Ghazal of the Cyanide Almond

The little cyanide almond exposed inside the peach.
The teakettle whimpering instead of whistling.

The pain of last week is gone. An earthquake has rattled Tokyo.
Someone is mowing, always mowing, slashing the street with their noise.

Before I was twenty I had no memories, knitting them together for later.
Dragonflies circle and tilt away like helicopters.

Or cutting trees, murdering trees, with that hoarse, slicing sound.
Last night a panther poured itself through an upper window in a house on
    a hill.

I lay on a big bed with a former lover, light slanting in like water.
You say your life is narrow, that there is no adventure in it.

A red geranium peeks from behind the sycamore.
Overheard on a television ad: "You can own a new solar system."

A black honeybee comes to my pen, drawn by the smell of ink?
One memory grows out of another, like a plant from a seed.

Fiat

After Li-Young Lee

Dreamed a rill that became a torrent.

Dreamed a woman who was my mother
but not my mother.

Dreamed St. Catherine's severed head in Siena,
trees bright against the haze,
the Palio a bowl bared of its tumbling horses,
the bright pennants and clamor of bettors.

Dreamed a fiat, *let it be done.*

Dreamed the stream purring under our bedroom in Vermont.
Dreamed a perfect sleep.

Dreamed a woman and a man dancing in a pyre,
so I could resurrect him,
so I could remember the spark.

So I could go in and out of the twelve houses
of the sun, the twelve houses of the moon.

And the man was not you; we lived in an alternate world,
and no one knew, not even you.

Dreamed the blue stars and the blue moon and the blue leaves.

Dreamed the world as a film
you can pass through like a ghost
and back into your life, inevitably altered.

Dreamed him. Dreamed you.

Sometimes an Angel

Rain pounds through the downspouts; we are all looking for an ark.
Lilies shine in the gloom and drink the rain.

Sometimes a person will return to your life
and remind you of a great hurt to your heart. An angel
inviting you to forgive.

And the rain sheds loud, heaving tears.

***

There was a time we didn't have a child and then we did.
It was summer; I remember driving up into the brown hills
toward Napa, a passenger, as the child was a passenger
in my womb; and I see that narrow road, scrub oak
on either side, as a border dividing my life into two parts:
a time of freedom and a time of never-ending responsibility.

***

A blurry figure on a bicycle speeds by; flooded earthworms
lie drowned on the walk.

Ghazal of the Broken Heart

When did I get used to it, the broken heart,
say to myself I'd rather live with it than die of it?

Daffodils and crocuses rise from their dark bulbs
with an inner glow. It surprises me

that Emily Dickinson is still read today and still
sentimentalized and misunderstood.

I like to watch the girl down the street glide
home on her bike, older and taller every day.

The sun at my back makes an animal of my writing hand.
Elms feather out new leaves but not the sycamores.

The calla lily is the most masculine of flowers
with its green sheathes, but then it opens, a hermaphrodite.

Love always has a vein of bitter ore running through it.
We diverge. The shadows are long. It is Lent.

Butterfly Wings and Honeybees

Butterfly wings litter the zinnias like tissue paper
unwrapping the gift, the body for the praying mantis.

You have taught me: this is the way of the world.
You have taught me to believe in God.

Black honeybees graze in the Rose of Sharon,
diving into its nectar, oblivious of the heat wave.

There is so much I have already said.
There is so much I have not yet said.

You make me want to write poems again.
You have taught me that we are human.

A white rose sends up a burnished shoot
where the blossom languished, crumpled.

You make me remember love.
You remind me of sweaty afternoons.

I did not know you then.

Identity Theft

1

Would they want to *be* you, stressed,
depressed, plodding to work every day?

What gives us our identity? Is it our family?
Our rebellion? Our accomplishments? Our failures?

Is it our language? Our loneliness? Our geography?

2

You are the fog; or
liquidambar leaves pressed between wax paper
at school, hung in window-
shafts of light. You are the child, the memory.

Are you the accumulation of your grief,
your lost loves?

3

I tell myself, "I am
eating oatmeal; I am walking, it's foggy, I can smell the sea."

A History of Navigation

Dark clouds shape-change against white clouds
like a Tuscan sky.

Northwest to Genoa where Cristóbal Colón was born—
we must translate everything.

If we had had an astrolabe, if we had had
the skill to stand on the rolling ship and use it...

We flew overland, separately, from the Pacific to the Atlantic.
In California hail flayed the already blooming trees.

The Portuguese peered across the strait to Tierra del Fuego.
They thought it was a continent, burning.

And I thought you were a continent. The Great
South Land, the mysterious Terra Australis.

If we had had a sextant or a quadrant, even
an octant, so elegant but so difficult to use...

Even Mercator's Projection would have been better
than the map we had of marriage.

You can get way off course if you don't know how
to accurately measure longitude.

God knows, we tried, gauging our speed by flotsam
rushing from stem to stern and a timer filled with sand.

We tacked in our sloop. The jib swung, it gybed.
One of us, or both, fell overboard.

The Dressmaker

It started when you were very young,
how you wanted to reach inside yourself

and pull out another you, a glamorous, wispy
girl of perfect proportions, to flesh out

the slender picture on the pattern envelope; you knelt
on the floor and pinned tissue to cloth, the gossamer

way it felt under your hands, imagining
the being you'd create. And later, after

you were married, the frisson of the fabric store,
your children playing amid the skirts of the bolts.

And then the suicide drop of your heart
when you tried on the dress, or coat, or pants

and somewhere, always somewhere, at the waist,
at the shoulders, across the ass, it didn't fit.

He thought you were fine the way you were, loved
your wide-hipped body. Only your body. You

wanted to open his khaki chest and find his heart.
Did it really pump red blood like yours?

He, he was perfect in every way.
And that was why you beat

your small and ineffectual fists against him.
But only you, only you, wept.

I've Known You So Long, I Don't Know You

On "Feeder" by George Fischer

You offer me half a peach
with its huge cyanide heart scooped out.
You offer me a red cabbage, clutched
at your warm coat's hip; your empty clothes,
a raven's feather pinned
nonchalantly to your lapel, ruined
walls behind you of some whitened hotel.
In my dreams there are always hotels, but you
are never there, I don't know why, you with the floating
accouterments of your jack-of-all trades:
scissors to cut me out
like a paper doll, forceps to pull me from the womb
where I might have liked to stay. Where
are you when you go away like that? Into yourself
and away from the house of love? You ignore
the tiny trees, you have no eyes to see them,
a green jalapeño, tantalizing,
balances on your sleeve. I want to say
I love you, you are so shy and open, your collar
buttoned against the cold, your gifts
so awkward and irrelevant, the way
you've always tried.

Scenes from Outside and Inside the Asylum

1

Rilke wed Clara Westhoff and quickly moved to Paris.
It was largely a marriage of letters.

October 1907: he limns for her a peeled
view of the city from the Tuileries after a storm.

The Cézannes in the Salon d'Automne that year
had irrevocably altered his vision.

May 1985: I write to you. Rain drips from the dark
chestnut canopy in the park of the Tuileries—

The Cézannes in the Jeu de Paume at the end of it then,
and when I step out onto the Place de la Concorde,

clouds parting over the famous obelisk, I know,
"You must change your life."

2

In his autobiographical *Notebooks of Malte Laurids Brigge*
Rilke rushes into the city like Flaubert to gather images—

the cobbled elbow of the rue l'Université,
the rue de la Seine, booksellers crammed into booths

with little stoves at their feet, reading,
happily selling nothing. Where I have walked!

Malte Laurids Brigge, insomniac, agitated,
walked for hours, walked all day, like

Rilke himself, to the iron-gated
Hôpital de la Saltpêtriére, once an arsenal,

where later Princess Diana came, crushed and dead.
Inside, repulsed, he took in the horrible

aberrations of those waiting for the experiment:
electroshock. And after being ignored for hours, fled.

3

This is where I lay the book aside. I walk
to the river: a hot day, about noon, a man and woman

sit in a car in a residential neighborhood,
smoking, the woman lounging

in the passenger seat, then leaning out
over the sidewalk to pull in the door, the cigarette

drooping from her lips. The man,
slouched in the driver's seat, shadowy, murmuring.

4

Gravel riprap, a breeze bends
a silver-stranded weed, one stalk in sun, the other

a negative of it, my shoes with their two dove
shadows beneath me where I sit

and the boughs of a tree construct a frame
for the slow, wide river.

This I can do. Watch.
It is all I can do.

Bernini's Ecstasy of St. Teresa

On the plain of Avila she could hear birdsong
and the clamor of dragonflies. But in her encounters
with God she forgot the sounds of the earth.

Bernini depicts the angel as Eros
with a wing at his back, a gold spear affixed
in his fist. He is half-naked, his right breast
undraped, and with his sweetest grin
he pulls back the spear to plunge into her heart.

She, enveloped in the cloths of her habit, the coif
and the veil, inches up from a bed of leaves,
eyes closed, lips parted, her skirt
in knives, legs loosened, splayed; she levitates

high in a niche in Rome, monied patrons,
on either side in their ceiling apses, voyeurs,
watching.

A fire enters her
with "pain so great it made me moan..."

Her bare feet swim under the movement of her hem
like carp circling a pond in opposite directions. She falls
upward, into the vortex. Into passion:

Christ's passion, which she has studied
in the abecedarian, the primer
of ecstasy, of union with God.

But it comes with a gasp
of the flesh.

In the Bleak Midwinter

(Italicized lines are quotes from *Leaves of Grass*, the 1855
edition, Penguin Classics 150th Anniversary Edition)

The humble gingkoes as in some crucible turn gold.
A calla lily furls toward heaven; the mandarins are ripe.

Let us go into this solstice with wood stacked, wine pressed,
the nearly obsolete fields surrounding the city fallow. A few

lights against the bleak midwinter, some song. But please—
no glare. This is what you shall do, says Whitman:

Love the earth and the sun and the animals, despise riches,
give alms to everyone that asks, stand up for the stupid and crazy.

Gingkoes reflect in the windows of a bus, an avenue, a tunnel,
bringing me suddenly here, now. ...*re-examine all you have been told*

at school or in any book, dismiss whatever insults your own soul
and your very flesh shall be a great poem.

It's December 8, the Feast of the Immaculate Conception,
which is not about Jesus or virginity, it's about being born without sin.

Yesterday buffeting wind and steady, gloomy rain. Today
liquidambars flare against an azure sky; they resist stripping.

I believe everyone is conceived without sin. The Feast
of Everybody. Red cyclamen jostle in a window box. Low-arced

sun stamps a radiant corolla behind the limbs of a bare ash tree.
Be one *with* the world, not one against the world, I say.

The gingkoes' leaves fall in one piece to the ground, enameling
and effacing the lawns beneath them.

Courage

A squirrel walks from the top of a bare sycamore
into a green magnolia.

The little phalluses of daffodils push up out of the cold earth.

When I walked out to get the paper,
I was surprised by the sun in the East
and to the West hanging curtains of fog in the trees.

Later, a man across the street
stood on the limb of an ash tree, sawing off the end.

The cold haze falls upward, out of the trees.

And now the full moon with its face on
rises in a lilac sky.

What courage to show one's self to everyone this way!

II: ENGLISH USAGE

Sword-Swallower

People are cynical; these days
they think the art of sword-swallowing,
like the art of love, is an illusion,
but it's not.

It is more than mechanics:
opening the throat, sliding the sword down
until the tip just touches the stomach
and the hilt
projects from the mouth.

It is fraught with danger. It feels awful.

The epiglottis at the back of the throat,
the peristalsis of the esophagus
work to eject the saber,
the kris, or that other double-edged
sword from Malaysia, the flamberge.

Bruises, cuts, even puncturing of the heart
(always fatal) are easily sustained.

Upon pulling the sword out, there is
the acerbic taste of zinc.

Oak Gall

> **For Julia Couzens**

You can see where the wasp,
genus *Cynips,* has punctured the bark of the oak
to create what resembles a walnut.

It's sometimes called a "gallnut." It's hollow—
not a nut, not a fruit,
but a wound.

The gall is seamed and mottled,
once sticky, almost liquid, then hardened, like blown glass.

(*Gall glass—the neutral salt skimmed off
from the surface of melted crown glass...*a scum.)

A sore, an abnormal swelling, a chafing.
Like bedsores, the constant harassment of rubbing
can kill.

It is winter. The scrub oak on the path to the river
is hung with the drab ornaments of gall.

The insect lays its eggs and the larvae grow,
enlarging the bubble,
"which yields the galls of commerce."

The new generation having left, the oak galls
become useful, so rich in tannin a bitter decoction
yields ink; or, in impregnating fiber,
black dye.

I feel the swiftness of the seasons, their hurtling.

Their gall.

An Anagram of Love

> "Monogamous voles depressed when parted"
> —Headline, *Sacramento Bee*

Scientists reap voles from the prairie
and watch them mate in the laboratory.
Monogamous, they are pulled apart as they bond,
a control group given a pill of forgetfulness
for the terrible pain of parting. What if
you were the vole? This would be a science
fiction tale, aliens siphoning you up from your car
on a desolate road, where they'd experiment
in their spaceship, to see where your sex lay,
your digestive system, your glands. You would be
angry and frightened the rest of your life.
Poor voles—the controls laughing like demented
patients who've forgotten the names of their spouses.
The others held upside down in water
without struggle; they would just as soon die
as to live unmated—sleek little mice stolen
from their love nests in the sweet prairie grass.
Soon we'll be given the pill too, never
having to experience the loss of love.
Who will write poetry? Poets experiment
only with words. I love words, for instance,
those that begin with "v"—voracious: voracious love;
verdant: verdant young love; village: the village
of fairy tales where the scrub maid marries
the king. And vole: the monogamous prairie vole.
Vole, you'll notice, is an anagram of love.

Praying Mantis

Our roses swarm with tiny green mantises.
A female grows large, the male small,
a conundrum,

her tearing the head from her lover like that:
the mating hilarious, "boisterously merry,"
with such abandon—

He seems to enjoy it more without his head.
(His brain is in his thorax.)
Sometimes she devours all of him

except the wings. She grows larger
and larger, brought to me
afterwards, lucid,

veiny and taupe, fixing her bug eyes on me
from inside the mayonnaise jar.
He has entered her totally.

Isn't that what you want, all of you?
As for her, with her haughty gaze
and enormous abdomen,

she's been released
into the zinnias, which are her forte,
and snatches butterflies from the air.

English Usage

Someone says "lucid," and I think of a curtain
that light passes through. But that's not right.
Lucidity = sanity, clarity. Translucence
is the curtain with light behind it, the half-
truths we tells ourselves. How much clarity
is there in a life? So many lies, opaque,
ebon, onyx. Shining lies. For how many of us
does the light burst through? Limpid
is sometimes confused with lucid, which is
a pool you can look into and see placid
coral fish feeding, opening and closing
their mouths, barely disturbing the surface,
as if tiny stones were cast in. A life
changes as you gaze at it: clouds scudding
overhead and disappearing, the sun flattened
by the shadows of unmoored bergs of cumuli.
Science has confirmed that time travel
is impossible. We can only go forth
from the strands we've laid, and usually,
like Hansel and Gretel, the line of memory
is made of crumbs. Memory is not lucid,
it is a prism; I've examined my life through it,
or shattered as through a kaleidoscope.
I may as well accept that all I have
is this moment, as I overhear someone say
"lucid," and then it's gone.

The Pink Violet and the Thesaurus

The oxymoron of a pink violet, which is not
violet (purple, plum-colored, magenta, puce)
or even a violet of the genus *viola,*
but an African violet, or Saintpaulia,
after Baron Walter von Saint Paul-Illaire
who discovered it in Tanganyika
which is Tanzania now, sits on a table
(a table is a table, a board, a slab, a counter)
and I am afraid (have a qualm, am worried
but not terrified) that it will die (perish, expire,
drown, smother, suffocate, close its eyes, shuffle
off this mortal coil, return to dust, cross
the Styx, die a violent death [see *killing*], go
west, cross the bar) from too much sun (Sol,
the daystar, prosperity, happiness),
too young (juvenile, immature, green, callow,
budding, unfledged, beardless, puerile)
and not the proper care (solicitude, heedfulness,
conscientiousness, watchfulness, vigilance,
eyes of Argus) (guardian of the heifer-nymph Io
to keep her from promiscuity) (promiscuous:
indiscriminate, mixed, miscellaneous,
confused.) You're not touching the word
"promiscuity" my little Roget; you'd rather
concentrate on death. And so the pink violet
is already gone (left, departed, withdrawn,
retired, exited, vanished, disappeared).

Necessary Dissonance

For Steve Coolidge

The piano tuner arrives with his ear and his fork.
He plays, fiercely, disciplined, the discords
of the untuned. I have forgotten the teakettle,
interrupting in unintended harmonics. He focuses.
He blocks. He loves the interior harp, the old strings
that he loosens and pulls taut, the screws, the hammers,
the cracked heart of the sounding board
which he mends with crazy glue—"like the old
violin makers." Across the street,
a contractor is starting demolition for a remodel;
two houses down they're cutting stone for a façade.
Conditions are not ideal for the piano tuner;
he locks me out on the porch. The upper register
sounds like tin; he bang-bangs the keys' monotone
and talks them down to warmth. The piano
is undressed, exposed with all its faults. He has
known it with its battered case for thirty years,
when we saved it from a honky-tonk life,
marks of thumbtacks on the felt. The exterior
is not what he cares about; he is like a blind lover,
knows it by its inner resonance, its touch.
At the end, he moves the piano's heaviness away
from the wall and back, vacuums the interior,
and sits down to play a glittering, rolling fanfare.

Rudolf Serkin's Hands

Like birds, like big fat birds, like pheasants.

Awkward, unbelievable, hunched.

Grabbing octaves, double octaves, easily.

Crescendo to diminuendo, in the wink
of an eye. A bird's eye, pivoting. Birds

lit on the keys and stirred them. Even there
under the balcony, each note rang true.

Beethoven. Beethoven's hands exactly

as he in his deafness heard: *agitato, con
brio* and then *pianissimo* and then

sforzando; his hands
were dragons singing; his hands

laughed, like water
tumbling over rocks. His powder-

puff hands, his cannonball hands, his
bowling ball hands, skimming the alley

suddenly from a whisper to a loud
glissando. A soft trill. His hands

the hands of a magician. There in the dark
in San Francisco. His old hands

like sausages, magic
sausages. His old wrinkled hands

blazing, like his eyes.

Typewriter

Some romantics still cling to them, the keys
a neck, a ruff, a mouth, teeth
clack-clack-clacking, stumbling
all over themselves, trying to write "l-o-v-e."
Love takes two hands. If you were passionate
or angry, you could bang your feelings out
like a piano concerto. The keys were round,
steel-rimmed like spectacles, letters slid
under plastic. They levered the keys,
which would tangle like stork legs.
You took typing in school
so you wouldn't have to look,
just touch the keyboard and watch words
appear on paper. The typewriter
was painted black with gilt curlicues, a loved
thing, an admired thing. A heft to it,
it wouldn't sit in your lap.
A bell clanged when you came
to the end of the carriage, *slow down,
slow down,* it said. You backed up and covered
your errors with kisses, like this: XXXXXXXX.
If you wanted to send your love poem
out into the world, you used carbons, black
or blue, and erased a typo twice, three times.
The keys banged against the platen hard,
leaving holes you could see through
when you held the paper up to the light.
You threaded an inked ribbon on two spools
through metal eyes; you had to get messy,
leave fingerprints. Some lead was chipped
from the keys, identifying an individual
typewriter used in a love triangle, a murder,
a kidnapping, just as a body
is instantly known by the cast of its teeth.

Dogs of the City

The dogs wait behind the windows
of the houses in the city.

The dogs wait
in yards, behind fences.

The dogs are like
that man with a strawberry mark on his neck.

The dogs are like
that woman dressed in black, licking her fingers.

The dogs wait on lawns
tied to trees.

The dogs wait at the end of leashes
at the end of the day, walked

around blocks; the dogs are like
slaves or prisoners;

sporting collars or little jackets, they wait
while someone scoops up their shit.

The dogs are like
Walt Whitman howling.

The dogs are like Allen Ginsberg
howling.

The dogs sniff at trees, at fire hydrants
and telephone poles

and at each other. The dogs are like
Tibetan prayer flags, flapping in the wind.

The dogs are waiting, they are waiting
for the revolution.

A Morning During the Tour de France

The day starts out hot. Someone is talking
about wine. It's cool in here.
A little girl with a yellow balloon
and a shirt to match, a pink bow and an aqua
gauze skirt, reminds my friend
of her childhood. The yellow shirt reminds me
of the *maillot jaune,* the yellow jersey
that appears on different cyclists
in the Tour de France, zipped up the back
to slip quickly on at the podium.
Muscles pump the differently colored jerseys
and ribs show through hunched backs, straining
through the Pyrenees, the riders focused, blind
to the beauty of the mountains; people
and motorcycles swerve into the narrow road,
and Basque sheep, bewildered, clamber
up out of the precipitous canyon,
out of the thick mist settling. My latte
contains a leaf stamped in milk. I don't want
to disturb it. My friend says "bizarre" and
"gentrification." The leaf slides down
to the bottom of the cup, intact, as I sip.
The woman talking about wine laughs.
She has perfect teeth.

Testing the Floodgates

The wild entrance bower to the café shoots vines
(can they be called canes?) every which way.

The newspaper speaks of floodgates
like a medieval city walled against the surge.

The word occurs to me: *insularity.*
Somebody says "exile," somebody says "ambrosia."

The floodgates: beveled timbers, a huge gasket,
giant turnbuckles. I want to use the word *recondite.*

They are playing "Celebrate, Celebrate," they are
playing "Bye Bye Miss American Pie."

In a photograph the gatekeepers strain to close
the floodgates, echoing Salgado's epic of Brazilian miners

stuck to the mountain by mud. A wind comes up,
the air is sweet. A woman walking by the patio

turns to her companion and says,
"I just did my little hocus-pocus and..."

III: THE SHOWER AT CARMEL

The Cooler

We called the pantry in the alcove
off the big kitchen
"the cooler," which is another name for prison.

The jellies in their ruby dresses, incarcerated
next to a sideboard lined with bottles
of gift port wine, lead-chokered,

that nobody drank. I would have
had I been able to locate a corkscrew
and figure out how to use it.

Instead, I'd take a jar of jelly down
from its worn pine shelf
and hold it up to the light, as though

I were a judge at a fair. We never entered fairs.
We weren't that kind of people.
We were city people with a backyard tree.

After boiling the plums, we hung the pulp
in cheesecloth bags from the knobs
of cupboard doors, where it drip-dripped

with a pond sound into mixing bowls,
its blood gathering over several days.
Then we tossed the flesh, boiling the juice

with pectin and sugar. The skins gave the jelly
its color, but were too tough for jam—
and we weren't jam people anyway.

The Shower at Carmel

We came every summer until we were leggy
and awkward and almost beautiful.
Running in from the beach, my sister and I
headed for the shower, yelling, "I've got dibs!"
Each of us stood there in turn, a fairy tale of steam
transforming us—steam and fog
had a commonality, both so different from the ordinary
world of trees and sun and blue sky and shops.
An ocean smell clung to us; we were sea spirits
in the shower, balancing on a slatted pine platform.
We toweled ourselves dry and became
human again, eating—even beans from a can
tasted like the best thing on earth.
Then we slept the sleep of the dead, of dead
children who always wake. A new day, a new world.
Our mother's one-week vacation seemed
like a whole summer, a whole
life, a Bohemian life, our real
mother. The musty smell when we opened the cottage,
the piles of comic books still under the window seat,
the orange burlap curtains,
the board-and-batten siding, Mother
in her pedal pushers on the rickety stairs.
I want to see it all again! I want to see my life again!
The mystery and the gaiety of it.
Our little striped swimming suits. The green waves.

Architecture

My mother built things in her spare time.
She could have been an architect but she was a writer.
In 1954 she flew to Japan, the only woman on the junket.
My lanky, mannish mother. On Waikiki for refueling
a man took a glamor shot of her in a two-piece batik
bathing suit, pale journalist's skin, cat-eye glasses.
She looks like she needs a cigarette. In Tokyo
she stayed at Frank Lloyd Wright's Imperial Hotel.
Carbons sent back to San Francisco read "fabulous."
Carved pilasters of black lava stone, cantilevered terraces.
He was known for his prairie houses, clean roof lines,
repressed chimneys. Suppressed
grief written all over my mother's face on Waikiki.
Earlier in the century the architect opened an office in Japan.
At home, his studio overlooking a pond in Wisconsin
burned and savaged, the arsonist hatcheted
Wright's lover and her children to death. His life
always hung in a balance between renown and tragedy.
Everyone's life hangs in some kind of balance.
The Imperial Hotel stood after the legendary earthquake
of 1923, phoenix in the razed city, swaying
on its floating foundations. In the carbons my mother
interviews Tonao Senda, 35, so lately
the enemy: "I looked up and I could see the B-29.
The firelight was shining on the underside of its wings.
It was beautiful," he said. Paragraph: "Tonao Senda
did not love the Americans." The Imperial Hotel
was demolished in 1968, as was my father. After two
weeks in Japan my mother, reinforced steel,
went on to Kyoto, Nara, Osaka and home.

Returning

It was only a rustic cabin, after all,
in the wooded hills of Berkeley. In photos

my father smoked a pipe, chocolatey tobacco,
glanced up from a typewriter,

his knees bumping a little round table.
We could smell tide flats, see a pinch

of horizon if someone held us, one twin
or the other, up to a window. We lived there,

babies, until we were three. They thought
they'd live a simple life. When we returned

there were cracks in the brick, columbine
in shady dirt under the firs, a basement

window sash raised with a bang, in anger
and surprise. The same droop of grape

for a doorknocker someone cared enough
to take a close-up still-life snapshot of

in the same bluish, falling-apart album
with the pictures of my father.

What would we be if we'd lived there longer?
Wild hill children? Fairy-tale children?

Is Everybody's Father a Fiction?

She uses a buttonhook
to close the grommets of an old-fashioned shoe.

This is long before your father,
but somewhere in the line, in Boston perhaps.

He takes off his fedora, then slowly removes the shoe,
a fetish, like a bound foot.
The stockings, the corset, it takes a long time.

He caresses the instep, the arch; the ankle exposed
arouses him. He or she fumbles for the garters.

A transom window lets light in high up.
There is a sextant on the table.
They are in the library.

***

Later there was a homestead in Ohio.
A pause in genealogy.
Your father is born in California
much later, on the grounds of a mental hospital.

He comes to San Francisco and meets your mother.
She kicks off her loafers. He puts aside
the Meerschaum pipe, peels off the bomber jacket.

He's going to write a novel.

Then he's gone. The thread lost. An echo

of the soft tread in pioneer forest humus
before the trees came down for light.

Your Mother Never Dies

For Jane Eshleman Conant

Red roses reach into the politics of the sun.

The sun is everywhere, like God. Like your mother.

But then it sinks and the moon rises.
Your mother never dies.

The satellites rise, rushing across the summer sky.

Your father might die,
but your mother never dies.

There is one white rose as well, humble, almost
invisible. That is you.

The street is still. Even the doves
have gone inside their twiggy nests, outwaiting
(outwitting) the heat.

Just the slightest wind shakes the long canes.

I smell the acrid freeway
and its eternal (infernal) sound like a polluted sea.

But also the new-cut lawn.

Your mother in your dreams with a ruby
or a garnet in her ear.

Never dies.

Fog

It's foggy and I can only be the one who sits in fog.
Yesterday seems so far away with its clear cold skies.
Far as the ellipses of comets.
Comets take so long to make their lonely treks
they don't even know they have relatives.
Like you, the young woman reaching me
from the abyss
of your childhood. Even though
light travels instantly, the incomprehensible enormity
of space has kept us apart. The comet, cocooned
and even gruesome (from *grue,* to shiver or shudder
as with horror) is like your story, a Hans
Christian Andersen story: the mother dies, there is
no stepmother, wicked or otherwise, only the father,
outraged, and his anger is your only orbit.
No one understands comets, and no one really cares
about the weather of another place. Elsewhere,
in the news, your fog is eclipsed by their blizzard.
You swam through a murky sea into my ken, or my
fen, like an object rising in fog, or a distant,
once-in-a-lifetime comet, pleading with me
to hear your isolate story. What courage a comet
must have! And fog, fog isn't darkness, but the soul
feels dark. You try to think, "It's sunny somewhere,"
but so far you haven't been able to believe it.

The Piano

The piano is on fire.
I am setting the house on fire.
I am floating
barefoot out to sea, pounding
like the rhythms of the sea,
wearing nothing but my slip.
Mesmerized by the sheet of music
in front of me; she calls downstairs:
"Stop that banging!" Beethoven
demands some banging, deaf as he was.
She has a migraine.
Oh, how I must be torturing her!
I don't care.
I want to slice through the silence
of this house, be an arsonist
of music. Music is my accelerant,
my sweet gasoline. Beethoven
my accomplice. "Stop! Stop!"
she cries. I won't stop.
I am an evil child.

Another Fiction

She walks out for the first time in weeks, feeling
ashen, feeling bandaged.

There's music in her brain but she can't get it out.
Some strings, some horns.
Ump-ah, ump-ah, ump-ah...

She walks past the fountain with the Gorgon head
like the headwaters of augury.

Everything is starting to bloom. The coral
crabapple, pure red of early camellias, and the creamy
calla lilies ready to unwrap their shocking golden stamens.

The old magnolia jammed with stars,
at first palest pink, then ragged white,
like a bandage.

A line stands out from July:
"A sudden terror of the clutches of trees."

But now the trees are bare.
Jettison the past, she thinks. *Immerse yourself
in the profligate odor of violets.*

And oh, the forget-me-nots, she forgot them!
Pale blue as the sky.

When she gets home, she's different, she feels
raw and new, the bandage peeled off
her eyes, her wound.

The Body of Pangelinan Cruz at Land's End

Discovered April 2006, San Francisco

There was no skull in the treehouse,
but skeletal remains
with some clothing attached. The hand
alone has 27 bones. Was it open
or grasping?

I see you motherless; I see you feral.

You disappeared into the cypress
weaving a floor of branches,
enmeshing yourself,
below Eagle's Point, below the museum.

Your work boots slung over limb-rafters,
text books splayed open randomly,
an ID in the name of Frank Pangelinan Cruz, born
Oct. 7, 1943, in Guam. Your sister
was looking for you, Frank,
since 1984.

The hollering of gulls,
their silver and white bodies reeling
over the Land's End trail, over the precipice,
the blue or green or gunmetal-gray depths,
calm, or, more likely, bustling with whitecaps.

You'd installed shades on your windows of air
against a pelt of wind. Your ceiling
the turning Zodiac
or the cold wool of fog.

You could have been dead for a year, your skull
bouncing down to the spectacular Pacific, the plates,
the closed fontanelle, the occipital bones
splintering.

I see you with hair like lichen, a raccoon
befriending you, stealing food
from the museum café, tarts
with fruit glazes, half a ham sandwich
on sourdough bread; the creature
masked, an offering
in the clawed cup of her hands.

You were traced to McAllister Street
but no one there could even imagine you.

You were traced to the swept plain outside Petaluma
where even the grasses are lonely.

I've been there.

And in the round drive of the museum,
the saltfish wind and pungence of cypress.

Remembering Carmel in Texas

1

We were invited; they were not.
Insensitive people who would not leave.
A late dinner, we finally crumpled with laughter
after holding our breath for hours, sharing
some complicated emotion of the grown-ups.

Geraniums in the fog, and banana slugs in our shoes.

In morning light, giant guts
of kelp piled on the beach, buzzing
with a net of tiny black flies, and the awful,
wonderful smell. The sea lion washed up on the sand,
that same smell, but more awesome,
its whiskers and its fly-blown eyes.

2

Reminiscing in west Texas. Brown hieroglyphs
of shallow wetlands seen from the plane.
On the ground, a hard north wind; we look up
at hundreds of Canada geese gabbling for order.

A suspicion of the outsider.

Plastic bags snagged in harvested cotton fields.
Time moves slowly as childhood here.
Sunset erupts from the rust-colored ground.

Through the Sealed Windows

Mistletoe hangs from winter-bare ashes like baskets.
The sky is layered into a blue and white parfait.

What would blue taste like, what would sky?
The smell of violets creeps into the house

through the sealed windows.
In a split second the present becomes the past.

The man down the street remodels his house
all through the stormy winter.

Hammering, hammering under the skin.
Roots under the soil, leeks in the compost.

Tulip magnolias peek over rooftops, their blooms
like fruit at the instant of perfection.

Then the petals separate and fall,
mauve and cream, slippery as memory.

The Week After Easter

Little spiky barrel cactus, three years old,
is blooming now in the window, silky

pink flowers closing at the end of the day
like ribbons in an old woman's hair

someone has tied for her in the nursing home
and they only point out her frailty. A haze

of dust in the atmosphere
whitens the sky at the edges.

Wind smashes everything, even ideas,
even desire. A possum lies dead on Riverside,

feet stiff in the air,
hairless whip of a tail and alien snout.

It's not playing. It seems exotic,
from another part of the world, like a kangaroo

or koala, marsupial and not a mammal.
In the same week a heat wave—we move through it

like swimming in hot water. On a crowded bus
a thin Filipino man holds a guitar

adorned with flowers and bows at the neck,
primly, like a little daughter.

Ladybug

1

Another day of fog, dripping
from an aluminum awning. I remember

the silver carapaces we peered out of
when we walked the fog-silent beach at Carmel,

plodding toward each other, disappearing
into alternate worlds, and the coils of seaweed,

suddenly, like snakes.

2

In the afternoon, the fog lifts. Walking,
I notice a ladybug on the side of a fence, awakened

early from hibernation. Once I came upon a river
of them like a seam of cinnabar, massed and sleeping

in a forest ditch, punctuated
each with their nine, or thirteen, black spots.

Refuge

1

There's a rotten apple in the fruit basket
and a wasp in the laundry room,
beating itself against old, flowing glass, the sash
painted shut.

I toss the apple away, otherwise it will slowly
infect each of the others;
open the back door to the sweet updraft
and usher the wasp out—*this way,
this way*—with a brushing of my hand.

The buzzing of fear, spiraling
on the troubled air.

2

Kim finds a hummingbird
soaked in a mat of grass after a storm, wings
pasted to its body.

Death is patient, but so is life.

She cups the bird from the ground, places it
in a muffin tin, the oven on low.

"When I opened the door, she was standing up!"
Oh, the happy
accidental refuge we humans offer.

The hummingbird tilts skyward from the lawn
without a backward look, clicking
a warning.

Two Weeks in September

There is something innocent about September light
when it spills down the gutter at 7 p.m.
We drove part-way on the piece of freeway overpass
where it ends at the river; twilight now, and lights,
blue and red, flashing. We couldn't tell what kind
of vehicles they were, but in the paper the next morning,
words: a rope swung from a cottonwood
up on the levee, out into the middle of the cold
Sacramento. I see in my mind the hole where you
went down, a maw right in the center of that wide
river. Then you pop up like a seal and your friends
laugh; but the next time you plunge
you don't rise. It was 5:30, 6:00 when they called
for help, 7:30 when we passed by, divers
scouring the river bottom; we didn't know this yet.
Your family had got there, the mood turned somber
and everything changed forever. The thing
about drowning is, when you're drowning, you
know you're drowning, but those on shore
haven't noticed. Drowning is quiet, and then
that horrible realization that you haven't appeared.
The river is close to me, your death was close,
but I will not remember it for so long,
not like your mother who sat vigil on the bank
for two weeks until your swollen body finally
revealed its hiding place close to shore, thumping
against debris. This morning sun reached
through the curtains and fell directly on the yolk
of my egg at the breakfast table, a fluke
of the season's changing, and I felt suddenly alive.

Chicory and Rue: Ghazal

On the sidewalk at 20th Street, a stenciled sign:
"Death to All."

This morning, meditating in the hush of clouds,
I began to remember when my life diverged.

A bell pepper from the market, each half
like the cup of an ear, lopsided on white tile.

Look how you clutch yourself
as if you could fly out of the chair in pieces.

Dry fronds of palms caught in the elms of the park;
mistletoe assaults the trees like empty nests.

The dead go fast, someone said—meaning
they don't linger for the small talk.

Mowed-down chicory, cornflower blue,
peers up from a triangular city lot in the morning.

Blood Moon Seen Through Cataracts

Each night the harvest moon
pours in, up all night with me
lopsided, crumpled
and scaly. My dragon moon
drunk in the quiet night, nothing
so quiet as 4 a.m. as we
contemplate each other, no one
between us, drinking
the night and its wonders, the silent
colorless trees, the empty streets,
no explosions
or chants of complaint, even the dogs
are asleep; night after night,
rectangles of light on the floor
and shadows of the mullioned windows,
the mysterious craters making faces,
stars drowned by the liquid moon
even as parts of the full moon fall off
and it's the gibbous moon
still bright, not quite halved.

The End of the World

In twilight haze a line of panel trucks,
billboard-sized, dream-like, stretch up Broadway,
the smell of exhaust and the Chinese Buffet:
"The End of the World is Coming Soon"
painted on their sides.

***

Once a scared and rash young woman
fell in love, then
inevitably fell out of love; she felt
she had to be wrenched through life, to feel
as if it were the end of the world over and over
for life to count.

***

Many years later:
slant shadows on yellow siding;
how pearly tear drops cling to the undersides
of rose canes and dogwood twigs
after an early December rain; how they
will not be dislodged and it is quiet
as snow; how cars swish down wet streets;

how sun whitens the angles of a tea pot
on a shelf in the kitchen window; how the trees
outside are bare and narrow.

Acknowledgments

Grateful acknowledgment is made to the following publications in which these poems first appeared, some in slightly different versions.

Caesura: "The Shower at Carmel"
Connotation: "Another Fiction"
Convergence: "The Cooler," "Architecture," "The Body of Pangelinan Cruz"
FutureCycle: "Fiat," "Praying Mantis," "Dogs of the City"
Innisfree Poetry Journal: "Parallel Universes," "End of Summer"
Lily Poetry Review: "The Dressmaker," "Two Weeks in September"
Montucky Review: "Attachments," "Ghazal of the Broken Heart"
Pirene's Fountain: "Sometimes an Angel"
Poetry Breakfast: "Ghazal of the Cyanide Almond"
Poets and Painters: "The Piano"
River Oak Review: "In the Bleak Winter," "Rudolf Serkin's Hands"
Stirring: "A Drive in the Country," "An Anagram of Love"
Tule Review: "Butterfly Wings and Honeybees," "Sword-Swallower"

Cover art, "Red Sun," by Dean Pasch (goo.gl/llxAKl); cover and interior book design by Diane Kistner (dkistner@futurecycle.org); text and titling, Latin Modern Roman and variants

About FutureCycle Press

FutureCycle Press is dedicated to publishing lasting English-language poetry books, chapbooks, and anthologies in both print-on-demand and ebook formats. Founded in 2007 by long-time independent editor/publishers and partners Diane Kistner and Robert S. King, the press incorporated as a nonprofit in 2012. A number of our editors are distinguished poets and writers in their own right, and we have been actively involved in the small press movement going back to the early seventies.

The FutureCycle Poetry Book Prize and honorarium is awarded annually for the best full-length volume of poetry we publish in a calendar year. Introduced in 2013, our Good Works projects are devoted to issues of universal significance, with all proceeds donated to a related worthy cause. Our Selected Poems series highlights contemporary poets with a substantial body of work to their credit.

We are dedicated to giving all of the authors we publish the care their work deserves, making our catalog of titles the most diverse and distinguished it can be, and paying forward any earnings to fund more great books.

We've learned a few things about independent publishing over the years. We've also evolved a unique, resilient publishing model that allows us to focus mainly on vetting and preserving for posterity the most books of exceptional quality without becoming overwhelmed with bookkeeping and mailing, fundraising activities, or taxing editorial and production "bubbles." To find out more about what we are doing, come see us at www.futurecycle.org.

www.ingramcontent.com/pod-product-compliance
Lightning Source LLC
LaVergne TN
LVHW020939090426
835512LV00020B/3427